A+ books™

Colors

# Yellow

## Seeing Yellow All around Us

by Sarah L. Schuette

Reading Consultant:
Elena Bodrova, Ph.D., Senior Consultant,
Mid-continent Research for Education and Learning

Capstone press®
Mankato, Minnesota

A+ Books are published by Capstone Press,
1710 Roe Crest Drive, North Mankato, Minnesota 56003.
www.capstonepub.com

 Books published by Capstone Press are manufactured with paper containing at least 10 percent post-consumer waste.

*Library of Congress Cataloging-in-Publication Data*
Schuette, Sarah L., 1976–
   Yellow: Seeing yellow all around us / by Sarah L. Schuette.
   p. cm.—(Colors)
   Summary: Text and photographs describe common things that are yellow, including mustard, pencils, and lemonade.
   Includes bibliographical references and index.
   ISBN-13: 978-0-7368-1472-0 (hardcover)      ISBN-10: 0-7368-1472-8 (hardcover)
   ISBN-13: 978-0-7368-5069-8 (softcover pbk.)   ISBN-10: 0-7368-5069-4 (softcover pbk.)
   1. Yellow—Juvenile literature. [1. Yellow.] I. Title.
QC495.5 .S3685 2003
535.6—dc21                                                        2002000706

### Created by the A+ Team

*Sarah L. Schuette, editor; Heather Kindseth, designer; Gary Sundermeyer, photographer; Nancy White, photo stylist*

**A+ Books thanks Michael Dahl for editorial assistance.**

*Note to Parents, Teachers, and Librarians*

The Colors series uses full-color photographs and a nonfiction format to introduce children to the world of color. *Yellow* is designed to be read aloud to a pre-reader or to be read independently by an early reader. Photographs and activities help early readers and listeners understand the text and concepts discussed. The book encourages further learning by including the following sections: Table of Contents, Words to Know, Read More, Internet Sites, and Index. Early readers may need assistance using these features.

Printed in the United States of America in North Mankato, Minnesota.
112012   007026R

# Table of Contents

The Color Yellow

Yellow is spicy.
Yellow is hot.

# Yellow can flower and bloom in a pot.

Sunflowers have yellow petals and green stems. The sunflower's stem bends to face the bright yellow sun.

Bees live in hives and make honey. Yellow honey tastes sweet.

Yellow can buzz.
Yellow can sting.

Lemons are yellow fruits with yellow juice. Squeezing lemons makes lemon juice. Adding sugar and water to the juice makes lemonade.

Yellow tastes cool in the summer or spring.

Egg yolks are yellow.
Female chickens called
hens can lay one egg
each day.

# Yellow sizzles.
# Yellow fries.

# Yellow peels off for a tasty surprise.

Ripe bananas have a strong, yellow peel. Bananas grow on trees in warm places.

# Yellow can spread on a thick slice of bread.

Milk comes from cows. It can be made into yellow butter.

More Yellow

A bright yellow rain hat helps people see you on a stormy day.

Yellow keeps raindrops from hitting your head.

Hard hats are yellow.
They help people stay
safe from falling
objects at work.

# Yellow is safe.
# Yellow is bright.

Most pencils are
made out of wood.
Many pencils are
painted yellow.

Yellow can fit in our
hand when we write.

Bright yellow lines
show cars where to
drive on the highway.

Yellow lies flat on the road when we drive.

Yellow is warm.
Yellow is alive!

# Mixing Yellow

Artists use a color wheel to know how to mix colors. Yellow, red, and blue are primary colors. They mix together to make secondary colors. Purple, orange, and green are the secondary colors they make. You can use yellow to make orange and green.

You will need

yellow, blue, and red clay

color wheel

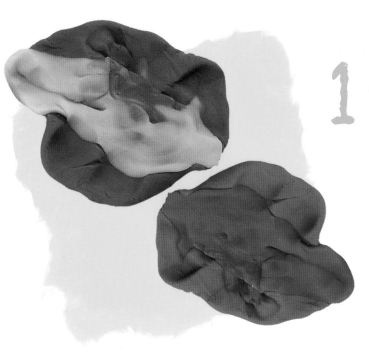

**1** Take part of the yellow clay and mix it with the same amount of the blue clay. What color do you make?

**2** Now mix yellow clay with red clay. What color do you make?

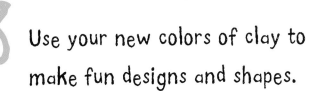

**3** Use your new colors of clay to make fun designs and shapes.

29

# Words to Know

fruit—the fleshy, juicy part of a plant that people eat; lemons and bananas are yellow fruits.

hen—a female chicken; hens lay one egg almost every day.

hive—a place where bees build honeycombs to hold honey; many bees live together in one hive.

juice—the liquid that comes out of fruit, vegetables, or meat

petal—one of the colored outer parts of a flower

stem—the long main part of a plant; leaves and flowers grow from the stem; sunflowers have green stems.

sun—the large star that Earth and other planets move around; the sun gives Earth light and warmth; many plants need light from the sun to grow.

# Read More

Borgardt, Marianne. *Yellow at Home: A Counting Book of Yellow.* A Gymboree Colorblock. Sydney, Australia: Weldon Owen, 1999.

Whitehouse, Patricia. *Yellow Foods.* Colors We Eat. Chicago: Heinemann Library, 2002.

Whitman, Candace. *Yellow and You.* My First Colors. New York: Abbeville Kids, 1998.

# Internet Sites

FactHound offers a safe, fun way to find Internet sites related to this book. All of the sites on FactHound have been researched by our staff.

Here's how:
1. Visit *www.facthound.com*
2. Type in this special code 0736814728 for age-appropriate sites. Or enter a search word related to this book for a more general search.
3. Click on the Fetch It button.

FactHound will fetch the best sites for you!

# Index